A PORTRAIT OF THE ARTIST AS A YOUNG LOBSTER

The Right to Speak, Sing, and Laugh

Written by Dustin Milligan • Illustrated by Meredith Luce

DC Canada Education Publishing

Written by: Dustin Milligan

Illustrated by: Meredith Luce

Editor: Leonard Judge

Copy Editor: Anja Pujic

Cover Design: Meredith Luce

Published in 2012 by: DC Canada Education Publishing

130 Slater Street, Suite 960
Ottawa, On, Canada K1P 6E2
www.dc-canada.ca

• •

Printed in Canada

We acknowledge the financial support of the Government of Canada through the Canada Book Fund for our publishing activities.

A Portrait of the Artist as a Young Lobster

ISBN: 978-1-926776-45-3

• •

Library and Archives Canada Cataloguing in Publication

Milligan, Dustin, 1984-

A portrait of the artist as a young lobster : the right to speak, sing and laugh / written by Dustin Milligan ; illustrated by Meredith Luce.

(The charter for children)

Includes bibliographical references.

ISBN 978-1-926776-45-3

1. Freedom of expression--Canada--Juvenile literature.

I. Luce, Meredith, 1988- II. Title. III. Series: Charter for children

JC591.M55 2012 j323.44'30971 C2012-901831-7

Preface

The idea for *The Charter for Children* first emerged when I was a student at the Faculty of Law at McGill University. After my first year of studies, I was concerned that the common citizen wasn't equipped to understand our country's complicated legal system—one that I myself had only begun to comprehend. Children are at a further disadvantage in this regard, as they have limited capacity, strength and knowledge of their rights. Combining these concerns with my love for literature and the law, I took on this large project—writing a series of books that offer children a basic understanding of the *Canadian Charter of Rights and Freedoms*. Thus *The Charter for Children* was born.

I would like to thank the Faculty of Law of McGill University, and most notably, Professor Shauna Van Praagh, who provided guidance during the course of much of this project and without whom the project would not have been possible. I would also like to thank those who have contributed their thoughts, insights, encouragement, time and puns—most notably, my three friends, Dorian Needham, Malcolm Dort and Josie Marks, as well as the wonderful team at DC Canada Education Publishing, Brad Ramsden, Megan Howatt, Meagan Johnston, and my incredible family, Keith, Deborah, Olivia, Christian and Jolene.

This series is dedicated to the children of Canada—may your voices be heard and considered, and may your childhoods be filled with respect and dignity.

Dustin Milligan

The opinions and views expressed in this book do not reflect those of the public figures or entities referred to or parodied in this story.

In a time not so long ago, in Shediac, New Brunswick, there lived a lobster named Aliya.

Aliya was an artist.

She painted some of the most beautiful paintings in Shediac. Her most famous painting was called *The Lobsters of Confederation.*

It was displayed at the entrance to the town's lobsterslature —where the politicians used to debate important issues in the community.

Aliya dreamed of better days.

Her small town had been taken over by a powerful group of lobsters who had claws like razors and shells like steel. They called themselves the *Lob-Mob*.

The Lob-Mob ruled the small town with iron claws. All the lobsters were forced to obey the mob's every word. Those who didn't were taken to a pot of boiling water in the centre of town.

And so Aliya and her neighbours lived in constant fear.

Mobster Lobster, the leader of the Lob-Mob, stood on his balcony every morning. He looked down upon the town he controlled.

Every morning, he would shout:

No singing, no shouting, no talking, or moaning!
No burping, no sneezing, and even no groaning!
If you should utter any such sound,
The pot will be lit in the centre of town!

And so the town of Shediac lived in silence.

Even the smallest of sounds, such as a whistle or whisper, were not permitted in Shediac.

Every evening, Aliya painted her pictures without making a peep. As she painted, Aliya dreamed of what Shediac looked like before the Lob-Mob had arrived. In the style of her idol, Emily Carrcass, Aliya painted beautiful trees and hills with the sun shining down on the town.

But that was all before the Lob-Mob had arrived.

Now, the town was falling apart.

The Lob-Mob had forced the Shediac Theatre to close. Roch Clawsine, who had been the most famous singer in Shediac, was now being carefully watched by the Lob-Mob to ensure that he didn't sing a note.

And so there was no more singing in Shediac.

The town's lobsterslature was no longer in session.

Frank Antenna, who had once been a popular politician in the community, was now out of work because no one was allowed to speak.

And so there was no more debate in Shediac

The lobsters of Shediac weren't even allowed to play their favourite sport—curling.

One time, a lobster threw a snail shell down the ice. When she yelled "Sweep!" the Lob-Mob ended the game. They took her to the large boiling pot in the centre of town.

And so there was no more fun and laughter in Shediac.

Unlike Aliya's vivid paintings, the sun rarely shone in the silent town of Shediac.

Every morning, Mobster Lobster would stand on his balcony and shout:

No singing, no shouting, no talking, or moaning!
No burping, no sneezing, and even no groaning!
If you should utter any such sound,
The pot will be lit in the centre of town!

One day, as Aliya was painting in Parlee Park, she heard a small chickadee singing. She listened eagerly and watched the chickadee dip its feathers into the Northumberland Strait.

Aliya wanted to hum along with the bird, but the Lob-Mob was standing nearby. She feared their sharp claws and the large boiling pot in the centre of town.

Nonetheless, the sound of the chickadee's beautiful songs inspired young Aliya.

Aliya wanted to sing like the other creatures in Shediac.

That evening, she used her creative mind. She splashed bright paint on her canvas. It looked like a Jean-Paul Rioshell painting.

As she painted madly on her canvas, she got an idea.

She thought:

> *We don't need to speak or utter a sound,*
> *To express our thoughts to all around!*
> *We can silently gather, united as one,*
> *To show the mob their time is done!*

Aliya was truly inspired.

She took all of her blank canvases and started painting every one of them. She covered canvas after canvas with her bright paint.

Of course, as this was New Brunswick, every sign was written in both English and French.

That night, Aliya painted more paintings than the Pod of Seven.

After she finished painting, she quietly visited every lobster in Shediac. In complete silence and secrecy, she gave each lobster a colourful canvas.

The next morning, as the sun rose and the members of the Lob-Mob emerged from their homes, the lobsters of Shediac stood in the streets as silent as ever.

But, this morning was unlike any other morning.

This morning, thousands upon thousands of lobsters silently held canvases in their claws.

On the canvases were written sayings like:

> *Lobsters strike back because we have our rights!*
> *The Lob-Mob must leave or prepare for a fight!*

That morning, as Mobster Lobster awoke from his deep, restful sleep, he was ready to shout at the town once again. He yawned as he opened the door to his balcony.

As he looked upon the town, he was shocked.

Thousands of lobsters had gathered. Not knowing what to do, he began his daily refrain:

No singing, no shouting, no talking, or moaning!
No burping, no sneezing, and even no groaning!
If you should utter any such sound,
The pot will be lit in the centre of town!

But the lobsters waved their canvases in the air—without making so much as a peep.

Mobster Lobster was furious. He shouted at the Lob-Mob:

Listen up mob, I don't care what you do!
Use thousands of lobster traps if you have to.
Stop this protest and all of these fools!
We are the Lob-Mob and WE set the rules.

The Lob-Mob was nervous. There were too many lobsters to control.

The boiling pot was way too small for the entire town. But it was the perfect size for a lobster bisque made of the Lob-Mob!

As Mobster Lobster shouted, the members of the Lob-Mob crawled away in fear. One by one, they jumped into the Northumberland Strait.

As the lobsters of Shediac stood on the streets, Mobster Lobster stood alone on his balcony.

He was helpless.

Out of the corner of his beady little eye, a teardrop fell.

The lobsters screamed with joy!

They yelled and yelled with their antennas held high. They picked up Aliya with their tails and started shouting:

We can sing, we can laugh,
We can speak loud and clear.
We can express ourselves for all to hear!

Gathering in silence was a great idea.
The Lob-Mob's gone all thanks to Aliya!

That evening, the Shediac Theatre opened its doors once again.

And just like before, Roch Clawsine sang his greatest hits. As the audience sang along, Mobster Lobster was forced to sit in the front row and listen to every word.

The lobsters were once again free to sing in Shediac.

That day, the curlers yelled “Sweep!” extra loud.

In fact, forevermore, as the lobsters threw the snail shells down the ice, they yelled “Sweep!” as many times as possible!

And so the lobsters laughed once more.

The lobsterslature also reopened. A banner was raised at the entrance.

It read:

> *There will be singing, and shouting, and talking, and moaning,*
> *And burping, and sneezing, and even some groaning!*
> *It's our right to express, our right to make sound.*
> *Never again will a Lob-Mob rule our small town!*

And so the lobsters spoke and debated with their antennas held high.

Later that day, Aliya returned to the park to work on her paintings.

Once again, the small chickadee sang its beautiful song. This time, Aliya was no longer in fear of the pot of boiling water or of the Lob-Mob's sharp claws. Aliya hummed along while she painted her newest painting.

She called it *The Loud and Liberated Lobster.*

Note for Parents and Teachers:

This story seeks to teach children about the freedom of expression, which is guaranteed by section 2(b) of the *Canadian Charter of Rights and Freedoms*. This section provides that:

> *Everyone has the following fundamental freedoms... (b) freedom of thought, belief, opinion and expression, including freedom of the press and other media of communication...*[1]

The Supreme Court of Canada suggests that the three primary justifications for protecting this right are the protection and promotion of (a) "the marketplace of ideas", (b) democracy, and (c) individual autonomy.

To better understand these justifications, a brief explanation is in order. Firstly, in regards to a marketplace of ideas, freedom of expression promotes the sharing of ideas, which allows for the growth of public knowledge and a more progressive and vibrant society. Secondly, in regards to democracy, freedom of expression permits a free flow of ideas, which is essential for persons to participate in social and political decision making. Thirdly, in regards to individual autonomy, freedom of expression allows individuals to express themselves for the purposes of mental exploration and self-realization. Each of these justifications assumes varying degrees of importance in different contexts.[2]

As demonstrated in this story, the suppression of free expression can impact all areas of a community's existence. In silencing the town and prohibiting sound, the Lob-Mob caused the community of Shediac to deteriorate. In forcing the lobsterslature to close, the Lob-Mob prevented the lobsters from speaking and debating, thus preventing a marketplace of ideas and the promotion of democracy. The Lob-Mob also prevented the lobsters from singing and laughing, thus preventing the lobsters from mental exploration and self-realization.

Aliya, in a colourful moment of inspiration, found a way for the community to express itself by abiding by Mobster Lobster's authority. As the lobsters silently waved her painted canvases in the air, the community conveyed its strength without saying a word. In turn, freedom of expression was restored in all of its forms (singing, speaking, and laughing), paving the way for the marketplace of ideas, democracy, and individual autonomy to flourish once more in Shediac.

It is important to note that freedom of expression is not an absolute right. Freedom of expression can be limited when the expression in question promotes hatred against an identifiable group (hate speech). The suppression of hate speech can actually encourage a free-flow of thought by ensuring that vulnerable persons are not discouraged from, or fearful of, expressing themselves.[3]

Questions for children:

1. Why did the community of Shediac have to remain silent? Was this fair?

2. Why is it important to be able to speak, sing, and laugh? Can you think of other ways to express yourself? How did Aliya and the community express themselves in this story?

3. In what situations is it okay to limit expression? When is it not okay?

---

[1] *Canadian Charter of Rights and Freedoms*, s 2(b), Part I of the *Constitution Act, 1982*, being Schedule B to the *Canada Act 1982* (UK), 1982, c 11.

[2] *R v Keegstra*, [1990] 3 SCR 697, 61 CCC (3d) 1.

[3] *Ibid.*